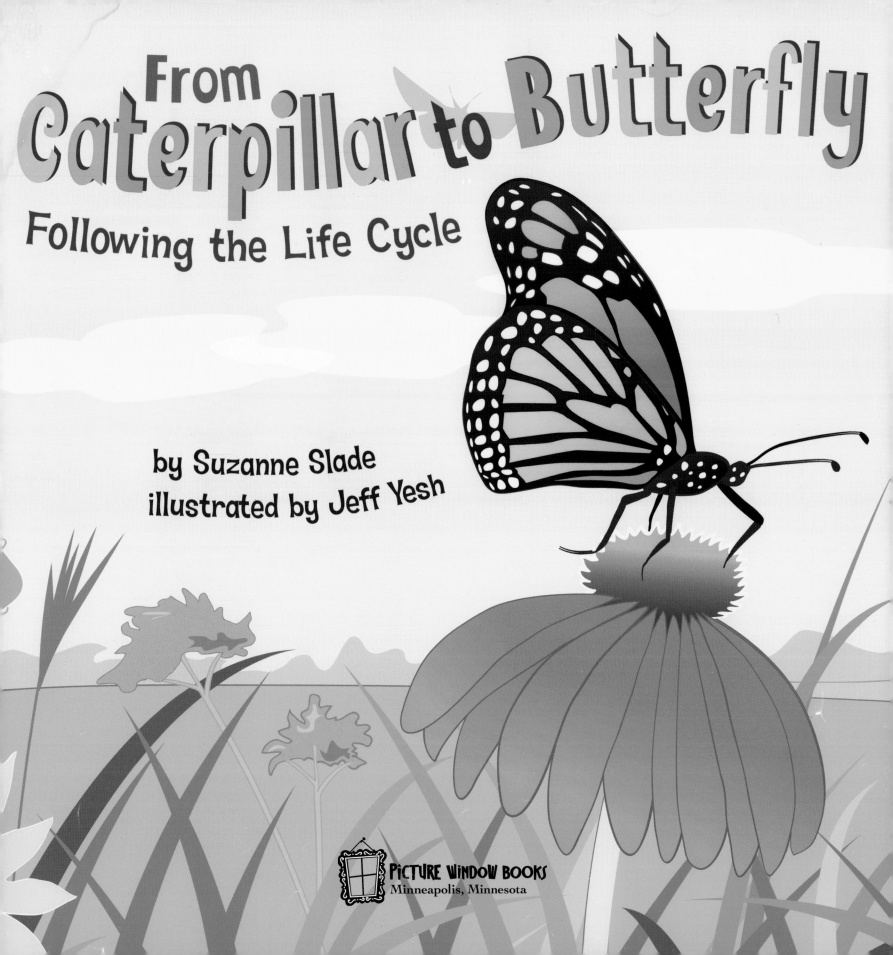

From Caterpillar to Butterfly

Following the Life Cycle

by Suzanne Slade

illustrated by Jeff Yesh

PICTURE WINDOW BOOKS
Minneapolis, Minnesota

Thanks to our advisers for their expertise, research, and advice:

David Marriott, Ph.D., Director
The Monarch Program, Encinitas, California

Terry Flaherty, Ph.D., Professor of English
Minnesota State University, Mankato

Editor: Shelly Lyons
Designers: Nathan Gassman and Lori Bye
Page Production: Melissa Kes
Associate Managing Editor: Christianne Jones
The illustrations in this book were created digitally.

Picture Window Books
151 Good Counsel Drive
P.O. Box 669
Mankato, MN 56002-0669
877-845-8392
www.picturewindowbooks.com

Photo Credits: © 2008 Jupiterimages Corporation, 23.

Printed in the United States of America.

Library of Congress Cataloging-in-Publication Data
Slade, Suzanne.
From caterpillar to butterfly : following the life cycle / by Suzanne Slade ; illustrated
by Jeff Yesh.
p. cm. — (Amazing science. Life cycle)
ISBN 978-1-4048-4916-7 (library binding)
1. Butterflies—Life cycles—Juvenile literature. I. Yesh, Jeff, 1971- ill. II. Title.
QL544.2.S535 2009
595.78'9—dc22   2008006451

Table of Contents

Colorful Fliers

Butterflies fill our sky with beauty. Some butterflies are large. Others are small. These insects have colorful wings that may have stripes or spots. There are at least 15,000 different kinds of butterflies in the world. All butterflies go through the same stages, or steps, in their life cycles. Let's follow the life cycle of the monarch butterfly.

The Amazing Monarch

The monarch butterfly is a strong flier. It can stay in flight for a long time without resting. Some monarchs can easily soar thousands of miles during a lifetime.

A monarch does not start out with its powerful wings. Like all butterflies, a monarch goes through many changes before becoming an adult butterfly.

Some monarchs travel as far as 2,000 miles (3,200 kilometers) to reach a warmer area during winter.

In the Beginning

Butterflies go through four stages during their lives. These stages are egg, larva, pupa, and adult. A monarch butterfly begins its life as a tiny egg. This is the first stage in its life cycle.

Egg

Adult Butterfly

Larva

Pupa

The word *metamorphosis* means "change." Butterflies go through "complete" metamorphosis because they change a great deal during their life cycles. Some insects, such as grasshoppers, do not change as much. Their metamorphosis is called "incomplete."

9

Tiny Eggs

A female monarch lays her egg on a milkweed plant. She usually sticks her egg to the underside of a milkweed leaf.

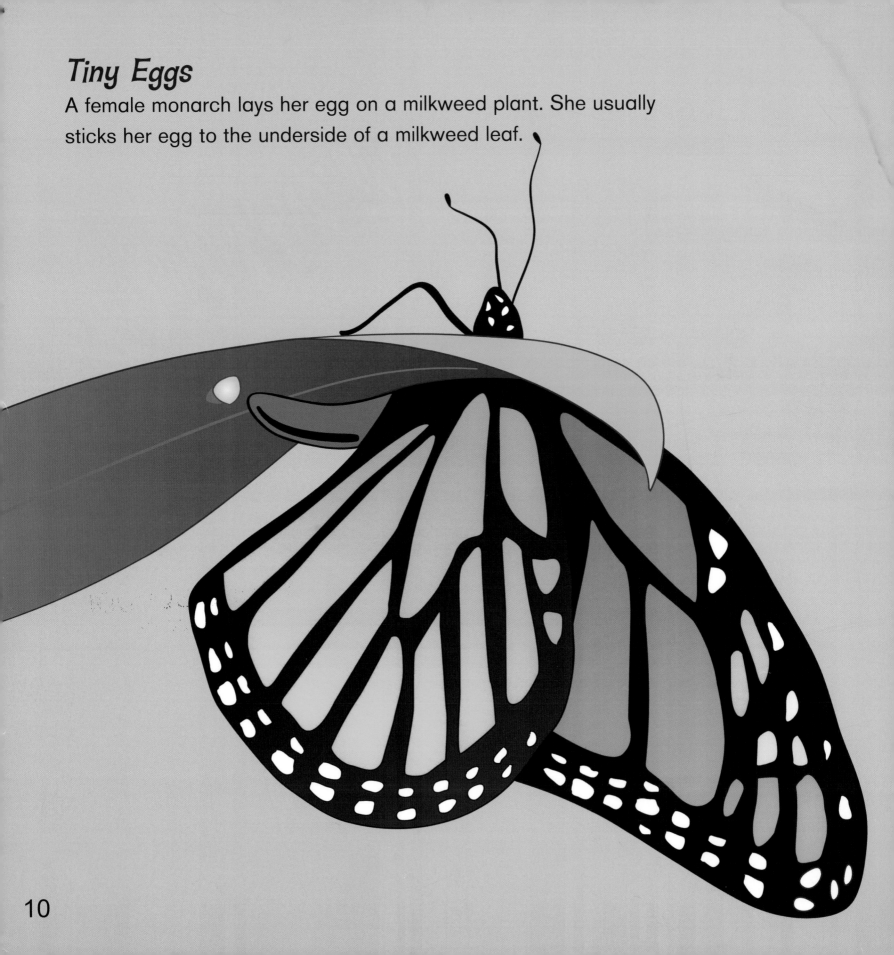

Soon a tiny insect begins to grow inside the egg.

Like most butterflies, monarchs lay one egg at a time.
An egg is less than 1/25 inch (0.9 millimeters) wide.
That's about the size of a pinhead.

11

Larva

Depending on the temperature, a larva hatches from a monarch egg in four to six days. The larva is also called a caterpillar. It eats the soft shell of its egg. Then it begins to munch on milkweed leaves. A caterpillar grows for at least two weeks. If the temperature is low, the caterpillar may take longer to grow.

When the caterpillar grows, it sheds its tight skin. First, the caterpillar attaches one of its ends to a milkweed leaf or vine. Next, the caterpillar's outer skin breaks open, and the pupa begins to come out.

Pupa

A monarch caterpillar sheds its skin four times. After shedding its skin the fifth time, the caterpillar becomes a pupa. The pupa covers itself with a liquid that turns into a hard shell. The shell is called a chrysalis. Inside the chrysalis, wonderful changes take place.

Once inside the chrysalis, a pupa turns into liquid. Only its organs remain. This liquid forms the butterfly's new parts, such as the body, legs, and wings.

Taking Flight

In about two weeks, the hard chrysalis begins to open. A new butterfly comes out of its shell. Then the butterfly unfolds wet, wrinkled wings. It waits for them to dry.

The butterfly has a proboscis, or long tube. It will use the proboscis for feeding. The proboscis is in two pieces. The butterfly must fix the two pieces together before it is ready to fly. After about an hour, the beautiful butterfly flutters into the sky!

The proboscis is located on the butterfly's head. After landing on a flower, the butterfly unrolls its proboscis. It uses its proboscis like a straw, sipping nectar from the flower.

Seeing the World

The monarch begins a new and exciting life as a butterfly. It no longer spends all of its time on a milkweed plant. Instead of munching on leaves, a butterfly flies from flower to flower. It drinks a sweet liquid called nectar. The nectar is found inside the flowers.

Monarch butterflies cannot survive in cold places. North American monarchs fly south to find warm weather before the cold winter arrives. Some kinds of butterflies hibernate, or sleep, for the entire winter. Others die because of the low temperatures.

The Cycle Continues

Monarch butterflies that come out of their chrysalises during the months from December through August live for only about a month. Those that come out in late summer or fall can live for eight to nine months. During this short time, a monarch searches for a mating partner. A male monarch often gives off a special smell to get a female's attention.

After mating, the female finds a safe place to lay her egg. This tiny egg begins a brand-new life cycle. Soon another beautiful monarch butterfly will take to the sky!

Depending on the type of butterfly, a life cycle may be short or long. For example, a short life cycle is about eight weeks long. A longer life cycle may last more than six months. The longest life cycle for a butterfly is about 18 months.

Life Cycle of the Monarch Butterfly

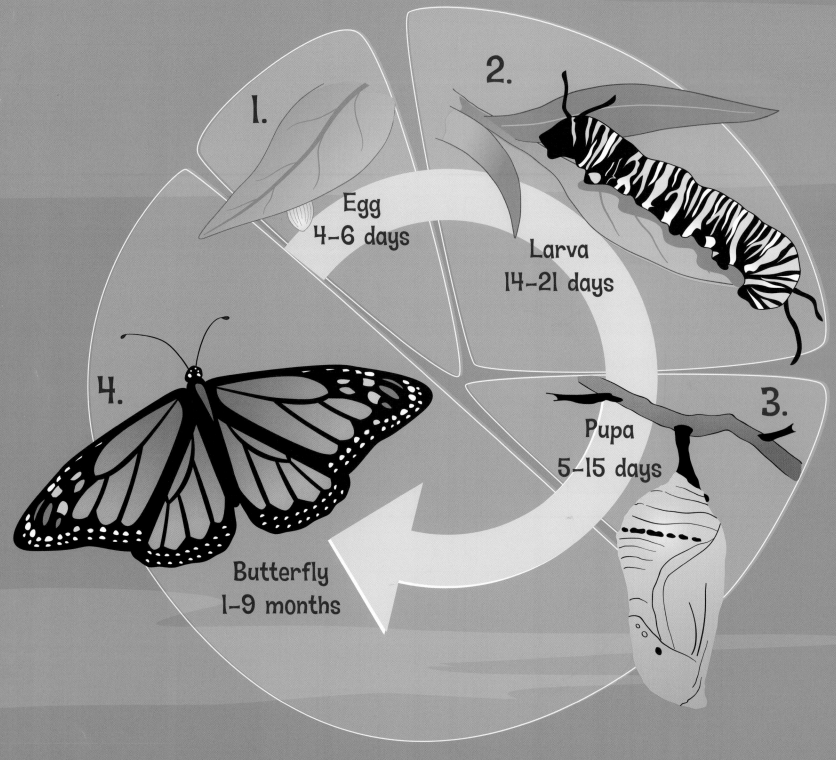

1. Egg
4-6 days

2. Larva
14-21 days

3. Pupa
5-15 days

4. Butterfly
1-9 months

Fun Facts

- An adult caterpillar weighs about 2,700 times more than it did at birth! If you weighed 8 pounds (3.6 kilograms) at birth and grew as fast as a caterpillar, you would end up weighing about as much as a gray whale!

- A monarch butterfly's wingspan is about 4 inches (10.2 centimeters). The North American western pygmy blue's wingspan is one of the smallest, measuring just 3/8 inch (1.0 cm). The Queen Alexandra's birdwing is the largest butterfly. Its huge wings measure 11 inches (27.9 cm) across. That's the length of a piece of notebook paper!

- A monarch butterfly may look like it has only four legs, but all butterflies have six legs. A monarch's top two legs are tiny and are curled up tight to its body.

- Some milkweed plants contain toxins, or poisons. After eating the toxins, a monarch butterfly will taste bad and will be poisonous, so its enemies won't want to eat it.

Adult monarch butterfly

Glossary

chrysalis—the shell inside which a pupa changes into an adult butterfly

insects—small, six-legged animals; they include butterflies, ants, bees, beetles, and flies

larva—a caterpillar; the stage of a butterfly's growth between egg and pupa

mating—joining together to produce young

proboscis—a long, slender organ that works like a straw; butterflies use it to feed on nectar

pupa—a butterfly's stage of growth between larva and adult

To Learn More

More Books to Read

Kelly, Irene. *It's a Butterfly's Life.* New York: Holiday House, 2007.

Loewen, Nancy. *Flying Colors: Butterflies in Your Backyard.* Minneapolis, Minn.:
Picture Window Books, 2006.

Watts, Barrie. *Butterfly.* North Mankato, Minn.: Smart Apple Media, 2003.

White, Nancy. *Butterfly Battle.* New York: Scholastic Inc., 2003.

On the Web

FactHound offers a safe, fun way to find Web sites related to topics in this book.
All of the sites on FactHound have been researched by our staff.

1. Visit *www.facthound.com*
2. Type in this special code: 1404849165
3. Click on the FETCH IT button.

Your trusty FactHound will fetch the best sites for you!

Index

Look for all of the books in the Amazing Science: Life Cycles series:

From Caterpillar to Butterfly: Following the Life Cycle
From Mealworm to Beetle: Following the Life Cycle
From Puppy to Dog: Following the Life Cycle
From Seed to Daisy: Following the Life Cycle
From Seed to Maple Tree: Following the Life Cycle
From Tadpole to Frog: Following the Life Cycle